WRITE!

YOUR GUIDE TO REVEALING THE WRITER WITHIN

ANNA BROOKE

VINDY TEJA

WRITING THROUGH TRANSITION

CONTENTS

Introduction	7
Prologue	11
Part One: Setting Yourself Up for Success	19
1. WHAT are you writing?	21
2. WHO are you writing for?	25
3. WHERE will you write?	29
4. WHEN will you write?	33
5. HOW will you write externally?	37
6. HOW will you write internally?	43
Part Two: Begin Where You Are	49
7. The Golden Rule: Keep it Real	51
8. Cultivating a Creative Mindset	57
9. Fear	63
10. Focus	69
Part Three: Continuing	73
11. Identifying Obstacles and Challenges	75
12. Creating Strategy & Possibilities	81
13. When in Doubt, Keep Going	87
Part Four: Completing	91
14. Re-Engaging with your Why	93
15. Digging Deep	97
16. Imagining the Completion	103

Conclusion	109
About the Authors	113
Acknowledgments	115
APPENDIX	117
Affirmations	119
Self-Care Tools to Support Yourself	123
Brainstorm Sheet	125
3 x 3 x 3 Content Organization Tool	127
Resource List	131

Dedicated to Inderjit and Lola, our endearing sources for love, solace and inspiration

INTRODUCTION

Writing is nothing more than a guided dream.
Jorge Luis Borges

If you want to change the world, pick up your pen and write.
Martin Luther

There is nothing to writing. All you do is sit down at a typewriter and bleed.
Ernest Hemingway

This book is written for you and for the writing you may want to share with some very lucky readers.

Are you looking for an opportunity to help you write, process, and document the changes in your life?

Are you ready to claim the major milestones of your unique journey?

Are you willing to give this whole "writing thing" a try?

If we were starting out on our writing journeys all over again, this is the practical and compassionate how-to guide we wish we had in our back pockets.

Whether you are seeking inspiration, direction, and/or support to walk you through the writing process, this book is your handy roadmap. Whatever stories you have living in you, they matter. We want to help you start writing them down!

A little about us: we met as writers, having both published our debut books under the same publishing imprint. We discovered a shared passion and desire to encourage others to write and engage with the brave journey of publishing. We began to collaborate and teach online writing classes.

Vindy's legal background and work as a life and divorce coach, and speaker, combined with Anna's creative and healing arts background produced a unique and wide lens through which we empower and support writers at all levels of experience. After some time, we noticed the same questions coming up repeatedly, and we realized how valuable a writing roadmap like this could be.

Write! Your Guide to Revealing the Writer Within is, quite literally, a product of its contents.

What we share with you in this book are the most important nuggets we learned about the writing journey.

INTRODUCTION

This book is intended for every stage of your writing. It is borne of our mutual desire to support creative expression, especially in the telling of your story. Use it as a powerful reminder that you deserve to show up for your own creative process.

From our book writing experiences, we know that writing through life's many transitions can be a deeply personal, rewarding, and transformative process. It is also one that can be filled with lots of apprehension and unanswered questions.

We both have extensive experience with the self-doubting voice in the back of our heads. It sounds like a cranky reality TV host: "So you think you can write a book?" Thanks to the tools we have gained to overcome that judgmental voice of impossibility, we persevered and each wrote award-winning books. We want to help you do the same.

We are here to embolden, galvanize and encourage you to keep going, keep writing, and persevere because YOU ARE WORTH IT!

We focus on creativity as expressed through the written word, but everything within these pages can be applied to whatever corner of your life that's calling for your creativity and vulnerability. Whether you're embarking upon the bold act of putting down your mark onto paper, a brush to canvas, or feet to the stage, this book is for you and your unique voice.

We encourage you to do the "opportunity work" found at the end of each chapter. Don't skip these exercises! They are the heart of the work for you to start, continue and finish your writing project. The more you engage with the questions, the more you will get out of this book.

You'll notice that certain themes and messages recur throughout this book. This is by design.

Our coaching, writing and publishing experiences have taught us a salient lesson: certain messages bear repeating…until they really sink in. These messages not only help silence the inner critic, they do a great job in countering the deluge of external messaging we receive about why we cannot (or should not) share our stories.

This book is divided into four different parts: Setting Yourself Up For Success, Begin Where You Are, Continuing, and Completing. We break down the writing process into key steps, sharing valuable tools that will help you establish and nurture a writing practice. They are designed to support you in overcoming challenges constructively, and seeing your project through to the end.

Use the prompts and guidance whether you are interested in writing fiction or nonfiction, a screenplay or a mini-series, a speech or song, or some other creative writing product. It all leads to the same result.

The tips, tools, and tricks in this guide are designed to get yourself out of a rut and put pen to paper (or fingers to keys!)

Remember: your story matters, and only you can write it. So let's begin!

PROLOGUE

There is no greater agony than bearing an untold story inside you.
Maya Angelou

We write to taste life twice, in the moment and in retrospect.
Anaïs Nin

If you think you are too small to make a difference, try sleeping with a mosquito.
Dalai Lama XIV

Everyone should write their story. *But I have nothing to say!* says the inner voice, or *Who would ever want to read what I write?* Or even *What if I'm no good?*

These are but a few of many resistances that can bubble up when we face our desire to write.

Every author faces these doubts, and those who push on through regardless of their insecurities or misgivings are rewarded with what lies on the other side of their resistance. It might feel hard, but it's not impossible.

Writing is a brave practice, and a vulnerable one too. It can be easy to come up with thousands of excuses when we sit down and start to write. No two journeys are the same, and your writing journey and process are yours to navigate, show up for, and ultimately follow through on.

This may seem terrifying, but in truth, it's a pure form of freedom that too few people give themselves permission to explore.

So why should you write?

There are a multitude of reasons for writing your story:

- Desire to write your memoir
- Recounting major events as a way to process and record them
- Record of personal transformation and/or growth
- Writing out family, life or cultural stories for successive generations
- To help, inspire, touch others, make them feel included, understood, heard, & connected

PROLOGUE

- You have a gem of a story hiding inside you that you can't wait to see in print

All of these are examples of why people start and finish writing, and all are valid. But did you know that there's one reason most people may not even consider?

Two words - Primary Source.

If you ever had to write a history paper in school, you may remember the importance of using primary sources. These are written passages that illustrate what that time period was like through the eyes and words of those who lived it first-hand.

Each primary source writing contributes to the worldwide library of diverse voices, experiences, and viewpoints that form part of the human experience.

You and your story are enough exactly as you are, and your story can contribute to a more comprehensive understanding of what it means to be alive during your lifetime.

Here are some foundational ideas that form the backbone of this book. You will learn more and practice each one, helping you build confidence and consistency in your writing.

- **Write about what you know and tell the truth.** It is powerful and resonant for the reader.
- **Trust your inner storyteller.** Imagining and developing your creative ideas are fiction and

non-fiction writing musts. Grant yourself permission to engage with this process.
- **Honor where you are.** Don't judge the conditions. You are enough. What you are writing counts and is valuable.
- **Come up with a strong WHY.** It will be grounding, motivating, and meaningful. Without it, you're more likely to procrastinate…or quit.
- **Get out of your own way and go for it!**

Another favorite technique we both use and love to promote? Self-contracts, which are agreements we create and hold with ourselves. State and write down your intentions, and let them guide your creative process. They can help to ensure productivity and completion of your goals. Here are some examples of self-contracts:

- I intend to finish my short story/article/blog posts/poems/book outline/book by the end of (date)
- I intend to write a list of the major turning points of my life by (date) and then unpack them one by one as I am ready to
- I will write a draft outline for my family story by (date) and schedule interviews with family members by (date)

- I intend to finish researching (chapter/article/book/writing piece) by (date).
- I will research and hire a proofreader/editor by (date)
- I intend to enroll in a writing course/coaching program by (date)
- My intention is to make a list of and gather the resources to move forward with my writing by (date)

You get the idea. The more concrete, time-specific, positive, simple, and realistic you can be, the more likely you'll follow and fulfill your self-contract. And you may just create some great habits along the way!

Coaching and motivational work have shown us that clients are way more likely to follow through when they've recorded or voiced aloud their intentions. Even if it's just one sentence long, that is enough. Write it, say it, and own it!

Kris Kozak, our design advisor and one of our most trusted and thorough editors, shared this simple but powerful anecdote about writing:

Decades ago I was at some party, whining that I'm not really crazy about my job, etc.

The guy I talked to asked: "So what would you like to do?"

"I'd like to be a writer", I said.

"Do you write?", he asked.

"No", I said "I'm thinking about it."

"Well", he said "Thinking about it doesn't help, does it? If you want to be a writer, just write!"

Author's Note from Anna

Many members of my mom's side of the family have written their own memoirs for generations. None of them have been officially published - they were all written for the family to know their lived history. I did not know the extent of the family tradition until my mother sent me the memoirs of my third great-grandmother, who was born in New York City in 1836. She tells of the pigs that would run into the streets after a heavy rain, picnics along the grassy banks of the East River, and what the rumblings of the American Civil War sounded like to her Northern ears. Her descriptions blew me away. It made me realize how utterly human she was, no different from me, and yet she lived in a world that no longer exists. What seemed normal and average to her would now be a freakish sight to me. Who is to say that my memoirs won't blow the mind of my descendants or provide deeper insight into my and their lives alike?

OPPORTUNITY WORK - QUESTIONS & EXERCISES

Complete the following sentences:

PROLOGUE

The reason I want to write is…

Something I have to share with the world is…

My intention for writing is….

PART ONE: SETTING YOURSELF UP FOR SUCCESS

First you dream, then you lace up your boots.
Portia White

Start writing, no matter what. The water does not flow until the faucet is turned on.
Louis L'Amour

With any new beginning comes an opportunity to create fresh possibilities. If we're ready to create more consistently, how can we set ourselves up well?

There are many ways to go about answering this question. We're going to break this down into WHAT, WHO, WHERE, WHEN, and HOW. If you are not clear on any of these, let yourself experiment and play with some new ways to set yourself up for success!

None of these are prerequisites to put words to paper. Consider them opportunities to set yourself up in new, well-structured ways to ensure your own productivity.

Please be patient and compassionate with yourself if the answers are not yet clear. It's good to have questions and curiosities. That's one step closer to getting clarity and motivation!

CHAPTER 1
WHAT ARE YOU WRITING?

I write to discover what I know.
Flannery O'Connor

Write what should not be forgotten.
Isabel Allende

Write what disturbs you, what you fear, what you have not been willing to speak about. Be willing to be split open.
Natalie Goldberg

There are many factors to consider when thinking about what to write. Everyone has their own goals and desires. Once the WHY has been identified as we explored in the prologue, use that to build out the WHAT.

Some examples of what to write, based on your intended audience and purpose of writing, can include:

- Memoir for family record
- Memoir for the public to read
- Personally meaningful letter to friends or family
- Position or advocacy statement to a public or private organization
- Private, personal journaling process
- Collection of essays
- Article or piece to be submitted to an anthology or magazine
- Short stories
- Poetry
- Television or movie scripts
- Songs

This is not a comprehensive list, so notice what speaks to you. Is there another option for you to pursue that isn't mentioned?

Sometimes we just need to start with an intended outcome in order to get going.

If you're unclear on the WHAT, that's ok! Just start where you are and watch what shape your writing takes.

If you're still hesitant about starting where you are, we encourage you to consider equipping yourself with some basic knowledge, conventions and tips about storytelling structure and writing genres you might be interested in.

Please visit our **resource list** at the end of this book,

where we have included some related links we love and use. They include brainstorming content, story structure, film and speech beat sheets, storytelling techniques, and vision boarding to name a few.

Author's Note from Anna

When I started writing my book Stripped Down: How Burlesque Led Me Home, I wanted to tell my story but also share what I had learned along the way to help others. No one genre seemed equipped to encompass the dual intentions of my book. I realized I was writing something that was part memoir, part manifesto, and so that became what I was writing. All it took was some creative thinking and listening to my gut to figure out what I was writing.

OPPORTUNITY WORK - QUESTIONS & EXERCISES

What are you trying to communicate with your writing?

What (if anything) are you trying to share or learn?

What structure or format do you feel drawn to?

What answers might you or the reader desire?

WRITE!

Write down anything that energizes or inspires you onto sticky notes and post them anywhere and everywhere to keep your ideas flowing!

CHAPTER 2
WHO ARE YOU WRITING FOR?

If there's a book that you want to read, but it hasn't been written yet, then you must write it.
Toni Morrison

If you want to share your work with the world, it is important and powerful to imagine and identify your audience. The more specific you are, the more animated your conversation with this group becomes.

Depending on what you are writing, your audience will change. If you are writing a personal memoir only to be shared with your family, that will determine the audience very clearly. If you're writing a manual, who are you writing it for? If you're penning a mystery novel, who do you envision wanting to read it?

In the opportunity work below, take a few moments to reflect on the many aspects of who you are writing for. If you're unclear on any of the answers, give yourself some time to think about it so that you can create clarity for yourself.

If you're still stumped, then perhaps the most authentic answer to the question of who you're writing for is…yourself.

Author's Note from Vindy

When I started writing my self-development book YOLO: Essential Life Hacks for Happiness, it was because I had had a health scare. As a result, I was eager to write a legacy book for my then pre-teen daughter. I certainly didn't want her consulting a Ouija board or Dr. Google for advice and answers on life. Yikes! Luckily, the health issue got resolved but my motivation for writing the book was amplified. I also had a desire to reach a bigger audience, one that included my coaching clients, family and friends, and the wider world.

OPPORTUNITY WORK - QUESTIONS & EXERCISES

Consider your intended audience and answer the following questions:

- How old are they?
- Where do they live?
- What do they do for a living?
- What's their gender?

- Are they single, in a relationship, married, divorced?
- What's their cultural background or ethnicity?
- What major life passages are they going through or have been through?

CHAPTER 3
WHERE WILL YOU WRITE?

[W]riting is real work, and chasing a dream of working from the beach isn't realistic or productive.
Rosemary Loshin

Setting your space can mean a few different things. It can apply to the physical space you write in, a certain intersection of time and space, or your mindset or headspace. Where you write includes considerations personal to you which can help create a strong container for your creativity.

Our physical setting can also make a big impact on our productivity and well-being. An attic may be deliciously private, but drafty. There may be a perfect writing nook waiting for you in your home, but nowhere near a power source. Your spare bedroom may be excellent, but what happens when guests come to stay? None of these challenges are insurmountable - you may just need to make some adjustments.

SOME CONSIDERATIONS FOR YOUR SPACE

We have discovered that when it comes to setting up your writing space, it is best to keep it simple! Clear or create a space in your home or office where you feel good. Creativity will flow more easily when the body feels relaxed and comfortable.

Keeping it simple also keeps procrastination at bay. The fewer distractions, the more productive a writing practice can become. For further motivation, you may want to place an object or two in your writing space that acts as a reminder of your goals, intentions, and commitment to writing.

We recommend that your new writing spot has:

- Proximity to a power source
- Supportive, comfortable chair
- Clear, stable surface to write on
- Good lighting
- Comfortable temperature

Some additional questions to ponder:

- Do you work well in coffee shops, nature/outdoors, libraries or other spaces?

- How much background noise do you need or enjoy when you're writing?
- Does your space preference change depending on what you're working on (writing, researching, editing, brainstorming)?

Make a decision and make it happen!

Author's Note from Vindy

When I think back to the practicalities of my writing space, I recall having to tweak my routine a few times before I found my magic formula - after I had torn out some hair in frustration!

I moved from my office space to my bedroom, from my bedroom to a favorite café, and finally from that café to an open and airy kitchen space. The kitchen island was big enough to accommodate my computer, writing tools, and resource materials. Having all of these items within arm's reach also gave me fewer excuses to procrastinate.

The result? A more "can do" environment that helped me finish a solid first draft. I still returned to some of my other favorite spaces when I needed a change or was engaged in a different part of the book process, such as adding footnotes, proofreading or editing. I tend to be a more linear and methodical person (yes, I sometimes think in flowcharts) so a set time in a space with all my "stuff" worked really well for me.

Opportunity Work - Questions & Exercises

Review the physical and practical considerations we've listed for setting up your space. Jot down your ideas and preferences for each one. What feels good?

Where in your living space is a good place to write? What about outside of it?

What else do you need to feel comfortable as you write?

CHAPTER 4
WHEN WILL YOU WRITE?

If you wait for inspiration to write you're not a writer, you're a waiter.

Dan Poynter

The question of time can bedevil a writer, so we encourage you to make a choice for yourself, give it a try, and see how it works. Any of these factors can be adjusted at any time. You get to call the shots! After all, this is you setting yourself up on your terms.

- **What's a writing practice you can commit to?** Is it daily? One or more dedicated writing days per week? Per month?
- **What length of time feels like a good place to set aside for your writing?** Fifteen minutes? Forty-five minutes? One hour?

Three hours? Notice what is sustainable for you. Set a timer, and stick to it.
- **Make an appointment with yourself to write.** Schedule it into your calendar and treat it like any other appointment. Respect it, and use it!
- **What time of day do you feel most creative?** Some people love starting their day with writing. Other people's creativity doesn't start flowing until later or well after sundown. If you're not sure, check in with yourself throughout the day and notice when it feels like a natural time for you to write.
- **Decide on a realistic writing schedule you can stick to**. Tweak it over time and as necessary.

We often think we don't have time. The real question is: are you willing to make time?

We encourage you to make your writing a priority.

Start where you can with the time you have, and experiment with what works for you.

Author's Note from Vindy

Once I committed to writing my book, I was pumped up and excited to make progress in a timely way. Initially I was quite unrealistic about how much I could accomplish in a short period of time. This led to some Be-Hard-On-Yourself-Itis, which was not so fun, followed by Reality Check 101.

Once I practiced various schedules and factored in competing demands on my time, I consciously decided to focus. Basically, I put the metaphorical horse blinders on. I settled on a four-hour block, three days a week, mid-week. I avoided scheduling client or personal meetings during that time.

While life naturally got in the way, and I couldn't always stick to this regimented schedule, the blocked time was the prescription I needed. I finally made true progress and felt a true commitment to my book project. Whether I was brainstorming, researching, writing, editing or interviewing, I tried as much as possible to stick to my schedule. The result? A solid first draft in less than six months!

Author's Note from Anna

When I was writing my book, I set myself a hard deadline to be done with the manuscript. I made the decision to write every day, but I didn't know what was realistic for me. I could daydream all I wanted about writing all day long like some windswept poet, but the reality was I had to find a rhythm that was both sustainable and productive for me.

I started with one hour which felt too long if I was having a creatively stagnant day. I narrowed it down to fifteen minutes which ultimately felt too short. I upped it to forty-five minutes before finally settling on a half hour. It was short enough for the stagnant days, yet long enough to get my ideas flowing. On the days when the muse was really speaking, I often went well past the half hour mark. There was something about those thirty minutes that felt easy and accessible with very little pressure. Before I knew it, I hit my deadline.

Let yourself play with timing and see what works for you!

Opportunity Work - Questions & Exercises

What is a time commitment you're willing to make for your writing practice?

How much time, ideally, would you like to write per day?

How much time, realistically, would you like to write per day?

Which time frames have worked well for you in the past? Or in other areas of your life?

What is a set up and practice that has NOT traditionally worked well for you in the past/other areas of life?

What amount of time are you willing to set aside every day to write?

CHAPTER 5
HOW WILL YOU WRITE EXTERNALLY?

When you make music or write or create, it's really your job to have mind-blowing, irresponsible, condomless sex with whatever idea it is you're writing about at the time.
Lady Gaga

The HOW can be one of the trickiest aspects of creating a sustainable writing practice. You've set aside the time, the space, and have everything you need - all you have to do is put the pedal to the metal!

Make no mistake - we are not here to tell you how to write! This chapter is about the ways in which you can write, including different tactics and styles to get to where you're wanting to go.

As you navigate the HOW of your writing, we encourage you to consider the following suggestions.

CAST YOUR NET WIDE

Don't limit yourself when it comes to inspiration! Reflect upon and play with the many creative tips and tools at your disposal. These can help you gather your thoughts and put your proverbial pen to paper.

Jot down ideas, phrases, and metaphors as they occur to you, whether it's in a notebook or the device you're carrying. We humans are way less likely to recall those lightbulb moments later on, so don't hesitate to capture your thoughts in the moment. Also notice where or how you might use these in your writing piece as this will also make it more likely for you to act upon them as your writing piece takes structure.

Perfectionism and creativity tend to hamper productivity. If you are prone to perfectionism, give yourself permission to let go of any judgment around the best or right way to write. There is no right or wrong way to write as long as you're writing! You might be writing letters or poems, real or imagined newspaper articles, essays or blogs, fictional stories or real-life events. All of these have their own format and you have your own style. Always remember that you have options.

If you need a refresher, we invite you to revisit chapter one for initial resources and tips to get started on various formats.

This need not be a linear process either. Write down any aspects, themes or scenes that pertain to your story as they occur to you or rise up in your mind. There's plenty of time and space to organize later. After all, the editing process is an ideal time to create an order for the flow of your words.

While you're in creation mode, just keep saying yes to the muse when she speaks even if it feels like the stories are all over the place.

STYLES

Whatever your mode of learning, processing, and synthesizing information, honor it as you write, and let yourself be curious about new ways to support your creativity.

Are you a linear writer, or more intuitive? Do you set out an agenda of tasks or do you prefer to go with the flow? Do you like to begin with a clear outline, or start from scratch and see where your words take you? If you're not sure, look at how you tend to approach, begin, and complete projects.

If you're unclear about what your work style might be, start with your learning style.

For example, are you a visual, auditory or kinesthetic learner?

- Visual learners see things and learn easily through visual examples.
- Auditory learners learn through hearing and listening to others speak and share.

- Kinesthetic learners learn through action and physical movement, using their bodies to process new information.

If you're a visual learner, do you prefer writing in a notebook or typing on a computer? Do you find outlines or flow charts helpful in making sure every point of your story gets touched upon? Do you write from strong images in your imagination?

If you're an auditory learner, try reading your work aloud to yourself, or read it into a recording device and then listen back to it. This is a step all writers should take, but auditory learners may find it an accessible and helpful way to move through the writing and editing process.

If you are a kinesthetic learner, you may benefit from using a recording or assistive device (such as transcription software) to get your words down while you walk, run errands, or move in whatever way helps you think and create.

Opportunity Work - Questions & Exercises

Identify your preferred writing and learning styles? How can you honor and explore these?

What are the fastest and most convenient ways for you to record your ideas, phrases, metaphors, etc.? What

HOW WILL YOU WRITE EXTERNALLY?

supplies or tools can help you accomplish this (notebook, apps, sticky notes)? Are there any new techniques or styles that you'd like to look into or learn more about?

CHAPTER 6
HOW WILL YOU WRITE INTERNALLY?

This is how you do it: you sit down at the keyboard and you put one word after another until it's done. It's that easy, and that hard.
Neil Gaiman

In this chapter, we look at how you treat yourself in the process of writing and the different choices you can make to support you in the writing process. Your internal landscape will affect your external environment, so we offer you some things to consider to create a calm, inner state for your creative expression.

SELF-COMPASSION

Start with a big dollop of self-compassion. The writing process is a vulnerable one. If you are writing about something that you've never written about before, or are experiencing lots of emotions and/or realizations as you write, take it easy and be kind to yourself.

If you're feeling stuck, or the words aren't flowing, be gentle with yourself. Energy and inspiration flow more easily through softness, so ease up on yourself and just let yourself play.

The creative process is a brave one. The word courage comes from the Latin and French words for heart, so keep coming back to loving kindness toward yourself as you write. Keep showing up with compassion for yourself, and you'll get to where you're wanting to go.

HEALTHY & REALISTIC BOUNDARIES

When we're discussing boundaries, we mean the external ones (your space, your time) as well as the internal ones (expectations, commitments). It's important to consider both in order to cultivate a clearer creative field for yourself.

Be protective of your time. Use a Do Not Disturb sign if you share your space with anyone who may barge in. Set your phone to a focus or airplane mode so that you can write without being distracted.

If you want to write a book in one year, what does that look like within a daily or monthly word count? What parameters need to be put in place to ensure that happens? If you want to write 50,000 words, what would you need as a daily/weekly/monthly word count goal in order to make it happen? Once you are clear on that number, open your calendar, schedule that time in, and use it as intended!

Writing about hard stuff? Take your time, and keep at it. Be gentle with yourself and write however much feels doable to you in the moment. When we write or revisit anything that carries a large emotional charge, the writing and subsequent revisions can provide a cathartic experience. This in turn can give way to more opening and resolution.

The creative process is a very personal one, so don't feel pressured to talk about it with others if you don't want to or if you're not ready yet. Your story, your rules.

A commitment is nothing more than a decision. Commit to your goal and show up for yourself, healthy boundaries and all - you're worth it!

REST

Finally, get clear on how you can take care of yourself and unwind after writing. Rest is an essential part of creation. Reward yourself with a walk, a treat, a nap, or any other way that helps you relax and decompress. You deserve it!

Author's Note from Vindy

One idea our first publisher shared with us and other female authors, is to bring the feminine energy into the writing process. You can do the same with masculine energy - or anything that motivates you and animates your writing.

Invite the inspirational or motivational energy of your choice in, let yourself connect with it, and notice what comes through. Ask it for what you need in your writing. Do what feels right and don't force it. You can do this every time you sit down to write.

Author's Note from Anna

Writing about the hard stuff is hard, period. I didn't always want to go in and write about the uncomfortable corners of my story, and so I decided to write about the hard stuff only when I had the bandwidth. By giving myself a break, it allowed for the stories to surface on their own. Before I knew it, I wrote for two days straight and all of the hard stuff poured out of me and onto the page. Take it one day at a time, and you'll get there.

OPPORTUNITY WORK - QUESTIONS & EXERCISES

Take note of the ways in which you can (or can start to) be compassionate with yourself in the writing process. Where can you include more kindness for yourself?

What are some healthy and realistic boundaries (internal and external) you can set in place for your writing process? What can you do to ensure your boundaries are respected?

What do you do to unwind? List your favorite ways of resting.

PART TWO: BEGIN WHERE YOU ARE

Not everyone sits down to write a book but everyone is a storyteller, in one way or another.
Charmaine Wilkerson

The scariest moment is always just before you start.
Stephen King

There's no right, wrong, good or bad way to begin writing. It just matters that you start.

Your story, voice, and experience matter. If you are writing non-fiction, you get to write your firsthand account in your own words. As we emphasized in the prologue, your written story is primary source material that contributes to a worldwide library of diverse voices, accounts, and viewpoints that inform the human experience. If you are writing fiction, begin to tell the story that lives inside of you, no holds barred.

No two stories are alike, and each story confers its own power, authority, and viewpoint.

If you are thinking to yourself, "Who am I to write my story?" we ask you in return:

Who are you not to write your story?

What you have lived through is more than enough to begin writing where you are, as you are.

What gets to happen if you begin exactly where you are with all the information and inspiration you already have within you?

In this part, we cover choices, habits and mindsets to help you move through any challenges as you build the foundation of your writing project or practice.

In short, start where you are, with what you have. You may be surprised and even dazzled by whatever comes forth!

CHAPTER 7
THE GOLDEN RULE: KEEP IT REAL

Fill your paper with the breathings of your heart.
William Wordsworth

You and your story are enough exactly as you are, so keep it real.

You are eminently qualified to speak from your lived experience.

You don't need a PhD to have made it as far as you have. No one is the expert on your life - only you are.

Write about what you know and tell the truth: it's powerful and resonant to the reader.

Think back to a moment when you read or heard a true story that struck you to your core. All that storyteller did was tell their truth. That's all you need to do in order to tell your story.

When it comes to writing, you are in the driver's seat. This can be both exciting and daunting. In its simplest form the act of writing is an invitation to you, an encouragement for you, and an opportunity to journey with you.

We recommend you avoid embellishment while writing down the major points, themes, and transitions. If you're writing fiction, then embellish away, but when writing about your lived experience, we encourage you to trust that your story is inherently enough. At the end of the day, it's your tale to tell and you get to do whatever you want. However, we suggest you play with telling the truth and see what comes through.

Another benefit of keeping it real is that it allows you to continually develop resource for your writing.

We are strong believers in the validity of the knowledge and wisdom contained within our personal stories. The wealth of our life experiences and the fullness of those memories are a resource for us to write from again and again.

So where do we start and how do we proceed?

To start developing your own resource library, we encourage you to jot down associations, words, phrases and anecdotes about the following categories:

- Loss
- Love
- Parenthood
- Childhood
- Ancestor stories
- New beginnings

THE GOLDEN RULE: KEEP IT REAL

- Sudden endings
- The first time
- The last time
- Relocation/moving
- Health

This list is a quick way to build and rebuild your personal resource library. The generative nature of this list ensures you will always have something to write about. We have also included this list in the appendix as a reminder.

So, if you find that you're ever at a loss for words, write down at least one association or theme for each of the bulleted points above. You will uncover a plethora of new possibilities for your writing.

Author's Note from Vindy

My book included hacks that helped me survive and thrive throughout my life, and especially during and after an extremely difficult divorce. I had to write the book in a way that protected my then pre-teen daughter, whose dad I had a co-parenting relationship with, and in a way that I was keeping it real so that I could connect authentically with readers.

From the get go, I acknowledged that I am no expert on their lives but I'm definitely an expert on mine. I also asked myself another critical question: Would I want to show any or all pieces of a particular story to my daughter, my mom, grandparents, etc.? If they don't need to know...then the public certainly didn't need to know.

I also had other options. For example, I could change names if I decided to publish my book. I could also access legal advice about thorny issues like libel or defamation, publication of private facts, false/misleading light, and other restrictions such as contractual ones or trade secrets. While these didn't apply to my book, I know other authors whose works did.

The point was that the information and advice was available if I needed it. These were not insurmountable barriers to writing my book.

In hindsight, I realized that awareness of these potential issues - and my desire to avoid them - actually helped me focus on what was really important: connecting with the reader about matters they grapple with every day, just like I did. This focus led me to only include relevant elements of my story, thereby taking the focus off "me" and putting it on the "we".

Opportunity Work - Questions & Exercises

What experiences, life transitions, topics, etc. can you write about?

Is there anything that you want to learn (more) about to better inform your writing?

What additional information and resources can you

access to enrich the story (e.g., interviews or research into historical context, geography, world events, lineage, etc.)

All it takes to keep it real is a choice. What is a new commitment you can make in service of keeping your story real? What do you choose to do?

CHAPTER 8
CULTIVATING A CREATIVE MINDSET

You need to learn how to select your thoughts just the same way you select your clothes every day.
Elizabeth Gilbert

Nothing is impossible. The word itself says I'm Possible!
Audrey Hepburn

This chapter can be summed up in four words: YOU CAN DO IT!

Embarking on any creative endeavor is a brave choice that opens you up to vulnerability and the many discoveries that come with it.

So how do we sustain our creative output? There are many ways and factors that come into play, but the most important aspect, in a word, is mindset.

Mindset can be defined as a set of attitudes or beliefs that sculpts the intended journey and its outcome. Whether we are running a race, moving through a huge challenge, or writing our very first book, our mindset will determine and characterize how we move through the experience and where we end up as a result.

As the Elizabeth Gilbert quote at the beginning of this chapter suggests, an important first step is to recognize that you can choose your mindset.

Secondly, become aware of what that choice can be. For example, notice if it is self-defeating, empowering, or something in between?

Thirdly, make the decision to consciously shift into a more empowering mindset.

Adopting an empowered mindset can be a pivotal step in addressing any fear that rear its unpleasant head. Many of us have a tendency to fall back on habitual fears and the stories they paint. They usually involve assumptions and information gaps, and often lack accuracy or even relevance.

The same goes for any creative vision, goal or venture. If we pay attention to our fears or self-defeating thoughts, we won't get much done. If we instead choose to adopt a supportive and empowering mindset, we begin our creative journey with all the tools we need to get going.

With this mindset shift comes power and motivation, not to mention an enhanced ability to counter self-doubts. The result? We are way more likely to be in a great headspace and heartspace to write!

CULTIVATING A CREATIVE MINDSET

Cultivating a creative mindset is a profoundly rewarding step of the writing process.

Creativity is the essence of spirit and no two creative endeavors are alike. When we choose to consciously cultivate creativity as the driving force of our mindset, we are saying yes to play, yes to experimentation, and yes to exploring brand new avenues of creation as a result. We are also saying yes to stretching our own creative capacity and showing ourselves how we can do it, in real time, one step at a time.

The objective here is to create, pure and simple. Instead of kowtowing to how things should be done, you are giving yourself creative license and agency to go to brand new places, try new things, and maybe even find a fruitful line of inquiry that will give form and content to your creative pursuit.

Some examples of a creative mindset can include:

- Believing in yourself no matter what
- Giving yourself time and space to create
- Being kind to yourself when you hit a proverbial wall
- Letting go of judgment
- Developing resilience in the face of creative blocks and trying something new as a result

Whatever the creative mindset may be, make sure it is one that eases the journey and inspires you to keep on going!

For some great mindset links that we love and use, please refer to our **resource list** at the end of the book.

Author's Note from Anna

Cultivating a creative mindset was one of the hardest and most rewarding aspects of my writing journey. Growing up, I thought that creativity was something to be emulated or imitated, but nothing that I could ever do myself. I learned the rewards of creative conformity, where my teachers told me to do something a certain way and would then critique my work. Talk about squashed creative license...!

When I released myself from the 9-5 work doldrums into becoming a full-time artist, I threw myself into the proverbial deep end without a life jacket. I HAD to cultivate a creative mindset as there was no room for imitation or half-baked ideas. My livelihood literally depended on it.

I was shown time and time again that when I took a chance on something new, on something that came from my innermost being, something that felt hugely vulnerable, I would be richly rewarded.

I developed a kind of creative resilience that strengthened my resolve to keep pursuing the weird, the unique, the out-of-left-field inspirations that would arrive, and follow through on them. There was gold in the "weird" or "random" ideas that would come through.

Adopting a creative mindset is what fortified my work and my commitment to honoring what comes through my heart and pours out onto the stage or page.

Opportunity Work - Questions & Exercises

What is a new creative mindset you can adopt moving forward?

Where do you tend to get hung up? What is a new choice you can make to move through the habitual blocks you are so familiar with?

When was the last time you consciously adopted a mindset that supported the successful realization of your intended outcome? What was it?

If you haven't ever consciously chosen a creative mindset, what are you willing to take on in the name of your art and your creativity?

CHAPTER 9
FEAR

Please do not feed the fears.
Unknown

We're devoting a chapter to fear in this book for a very good reason: it's one of the most annoying and recurring demotivators on the writing journey!

It's important to distinguish between fear and danger. Danger is real. It's the real possibility of suffering harm or injury, and such threats and risks need to be dealt with. Fears, on the other hand, live mainly in our head and hearts. That can make them feel real.

You may have heard of the acronym FEAR, which stands for False Evidence Appearing Real. For as scary and real-feeling our fears may be when it comes to creative expression, it's important to shine some light onto them in order to see them for what they are and dispel them one at a time.

As we like to say, there are more fears out there than ice cream flavors. Here's a sampling of some fears we have come across ourselves:

- Failure
- Criticism
- Rejection
- Disappointment
- Miserable
- Loneliness
- The Unknown
- Not knowing enough
- Not having enough to say

What would it feel like to have all of these fears be gone from your heart and head? What becomes possible as a result?

Food for thought: What if what you're scared of is actually a huge blinking neon sign that is pointing you to do whatever it is that you're scared of? In this scenario, the acronym FEAR becomes something entirely different: Face Everything and Recover.

Another thing we've found invaluable when trying to overcome our fears - whether in life or just with our writing - is to invoke a well-timed affirmation or two. We have included a list of some helpful affirmations in the **Appendix**.

FEAR

Author's Note from Vindy

As a life and divorce coach, I find it's common to come up against a client's limiting beliefs and fears, especially as they work towards their goals and vision. In my book YOLO, I share a few benefits of overcoming your fears, and am sharing them below. I encourage you to apply them to your writing journey.

- *Fears limit or even stop you from trying new things, exploring different solutions and discovering new things about yourself and the world. Fears are really opportunities for growth and learning, especially in a safe and supportive environment.*
- *Fears encourage you to make assumptions, take things personally and generally "play a movie" in your head, which may or may not even be accurate or relevant.*
- *Feelings of fear are messages you get from your brain and nervous system. They're a normal part of life, and what you do with them is what matters. Ignoring them altogether can obviously lead to bad outcomes. On the other hand, allowing them to dominate your thoughts and actions often makes things way worse.*

When I finished the first draft of my book, I hosted a focus group. It included people I respected and trusted. Some had written and published books themselves, others worked in communications, while some were self-growth book enthusiasts.

I was rather proud of how intentional and proactive I was. That feeling was short lived once all the feedback started rolling in! My worst fears around failure, criticism, and not knowing enough erupted to the surface as the group bombarded me with questions, suggestions and perspectives that I hadn't fully considered before.

Luckily one of the members who sensed my overwhelm followed up later to share some salient facts with me.

Firstly, I had written an entire first draft of a book and was actively pursuing next steps, something so many others just dream or talk about.

Secondly, the group hadn't read my book! I was not ready to be that vulnerable yet. Their remarks and questions were based on limited information I had shared.

Lastly, she asked me what I would say to a coaching client who was in a similar situation? Whoa! That was the question that rekindled my motivation and drive to finish the project. It reminded me that my fears were really living in my head, and that I was more than qualified to write such a book.

I could use the questions and feedback to get clearer on the book's purpose as well as add content and edits that could help me reach a much wider audience. Whew! What initially seemed like focus group "shock therapy" was really a gift that allowed me to face my fears and refocus in productive ways.

Opportunity Work - Questions & Exercises

Review the Fears List in this chapter and note which ones you've encountered in relation to your creative process. Feel free to add any additional ones not mentioned.

For each fear you identified, consider what untested assumptions or information gaps might be present (e.g., If I fail to write more than one sentence per day, I am no good at writing. OR If I don't know enough about a certain historical event, I can't write about this.)?

How might you be able to reframe some or all of the fears in service of your writing? (e.g., Each sentence I write is one step closer to clarity and completion. OR I am willing to learn more about the historical moment I am writing about in order to be more fully informed.)

All it takes to keep writing is a choice. What is a new commitment you can make in service of your writing practice? So, what do you choose to do?

CHAPTER 10
FOCUS

I don't fear the man who knows 10,000 kicks. I fear the man who has practiced the same kick 10,000 times.

Bruce Lee

So how do you counteract your fears in order to create? In a word: focus.

In our writing workshops, we often talk about focus as our favorite antidote to fear. When you bring focus to any situation, you automatically zero in on what's important and why, rather than worrying about what may or may not happen afterwards.

This allows you to strategize around your fears in practical, effective, and personally meaningful ways.

In their book *The One Thing*, authors Gary Keller and Jay Papasan speak about the word "priority". In our modern culture, it is often pluralized which in truth is a maladaptation of the word and concept. The word priority is derived from the Latin *prioritas* which means first in rank or order. The word itself is singular, as there can only be one item, thought, or goal in the first place.

Instead of confusing ourselves and overloading our proverbial plates with multiple, competing points of focus, take a moment to think about the most important thing that you want to focus on.

We can have multiple areas of interest or creative destinations, but it is much more efficient to concentrate your creative flow in a single stream. To use an analogy, it is more productive to grow a foot in one direction instead of one inch in twelve directions.

By focusing on a sole aspect or task, you walk and write with completion in mind. When the primary focus is complete, you can move onto the next one.

Developing focus is also an effective way to clear our creative pathways and concentrate our energies into creating major themes, individual sections, and consistently building content.

Author's Note from Anna

I historically have had a very hard time focusing. My favorite explanation for how my mind works is like a goat on roller skates - loud and all over the place. When it came time to write my book, I knew I needed to develop some new habits that would help me reach the finish line. So, I asked myself each time I sat down to write what my top priority was, and I would focus on it until either the task was done or I was. I rarely did more than I had set out to do at the start of any writing session - if I was to remain engaged and focused, I had to have very clear limits for myself so I didn't get burnt out.

Some days it felt impossible to focus on just one thing. Other days it felt like a godsend. No matter what it felt like, I kept showing up, choosing one thing to focus on, and writing about that and only that.

Before I knew it, my first full draft was done, and soon thereafter the final manuscript. I even impressed myself! It was an incredibly satisfying experience. I realized that whatever I put my mind to, all I needed was focus and I'd be off to the races.

Opportunity Work - Questions & Exercises

Ask yourself what the most important thing is for you to focus on. Choose whichever is the loudest in you, and focus on it. Set a timer if need be, but give yourself to the task and avoid any distraction.

What can you focus on in the following: your writing, your process, your story, what you want to share, your desired learning, etc.

What's something you can do to optimally set up your

writing space to be free from distraction? (office space, programs, apps, supplies)?

What kind of accountability system could you consider and/or add (writing buddy, online or in-person writing group, etc.)?

All it takes to keep writing is a choice. What is a new commitment you can make in service of your writing practice? So, what do you choose to do?

PART THREE: CONTINUING

A word after a word after a word is power.
Margaret Atwood

The space in between beginning your book and finishing it requires commitment, consistency, and the will to keep showing up to your writing all the way through to its completion. After all, it's your story. If you don't show up to put those words down onto paper, who will?

Everyone writes differently, and for some people, the journey of writing can be a delicious escape or memory-filled trip into the past. For others, showing up to a regular writing practice may feel like a feat of Herculean strength.

No matter your relationship to the act of continuing, it's a crucial part of the brave journey of writing and more importantly, the successful completion of your piece.

In this part, we get into the nitty gritty of continuing through the creative process. We explore identifying obstacles and challenges that may feel like familiar stumbling blocks, creating strategies to ensure fluid productivity, and whenever doubt arises, to keep writing!

Author's Note from Anna

If you haven't already, I suggest you become your own ally in this process of creative self-expression. I used to be incredibly hard on myself when it came to any creative endeavor. I learned that writing could be fun if I just gave myself a break and chose to be kind to myself. That one small decision was a game changer. Instead of writing against my inner editor and foul judge, I realized that I could show up and just play, letting the words flow out however they wanted to. By changing my mindset and loosening up my self-judgment, writing became much more enjoyable and productive.

CHAPTER 11
IDENTIFYING OBSTACLES AND CHALLENGES

The pursuit of excellence is gratifying and healthy. The pursuit of perfection is frustrating, neurotic, and a terrible waste of time.
Edwin Bliss

The truth will set you free. But first it will piss you off.
Gloria Steinem

As you buckle in and venture onto the writing road, let's take some time to address the speed bumps and potholes, aka obstacles and challenges you may encounter along the way. We want you to have readily accessible tools in your creatively empowered toolbox!

Obstacles and challenges can have a stubborn power to get in our way of everything, including our writing. It's worthwhile to identify what's going on behind the scenes so you can gain clarity about what might be really holding you back.

When you shine light onto a shadow, it disappears. The same can apply to the creative challenges we experience.

Common obstacles that can come up include:

- Overwhelm
- Blocks, slumps or chokes
- Shame
- Judgment
- Fears
- Doubt, uncertainty, hesitation
- Perfectionism
- Procrastination

We appreciate that any inspiration - no matter how strongly felt - can also quickly morph into project paralysis. As with any creative undertaking, you may find yourself grappling with a cornucopia of obstacles and challenges that hamper your progress.

Believe us, we have definitely been there. You're not alone if that happens.

Naming whatever the obstacle you're encountering is the first step. Once you have clarity about them, you can start to formulate a strategy to ensure they don't hold you back.

Author's Note from Anna

I was too convinced of my own weakness in the face of big obstacles when I was first starting out. After some time, I learned to dive into the thoughts and feelings behind each obstacle and uncover what the root thoughts were. Often, whatever was bugging me was rooted in enoughness - I wasn't smart enough, didn't have the right words, was lacking in know-how, etc. I started to affirm that I had everything I needed to do whatever it was I wanted to do. That thought created a shift that in turn produced incredible momentum that propelled me forward seemingly without effort.

There was also a part of me that was very attached to the outcome I had in mind. I was attached to the very precise way I imagined I needed to achieve it. I had to soften my attachment to the "how" and instead hold a soft focus on the intended outcome without any rigidity or gripping. The softness allowed me to create more space, which in turn created new possibilities that I hadn't considered before. The minute I let go of the need to do it all perfectly and in a certain way, the process got easier and, dare I say, fun!

This is not to say I banished obstacles from my life - far from it. I have found wonderful resources in coming back to these tools and doing what I can with what I have, which thank goodness is enough!

Author's Note from Vindy

I had a plethora of obstacles and challenges that made

guest appearances on my writing journey. A recurring one was the sense of overwhelm.

Overwhelmed by all the steps it takes to write a book: research, writing, editing, formatting, publishing, and marketing. Overwhelmed by all the choices, resources and services that exist within each of those activities. Overwhelmed by how exhaustive I thought I had to be on each topic in the book. Overwhelmed by being overwhelmed. You get the idea.

My "symptoms" were varied: impatience, testiness, tension in my shoulders and back, and fatigue. I would either procrastinate and come up with clever rationalizations about why I couldn't or shouldn't write at that moment, or I'd engage in over researching and overthinking. Oh yes, and I'd organize and clean. The house was never tidier and more in order than when I was writing my book!

The choice I made was very simple, though by no means small. It was also very much connected to my sense of self-respect. What I chose to do was keep showing up and doing the next right thing, the next right thing, and so on, no matter how hard it seemed to be at the time. It meant not cutting corners and not waiting for outside validation or prompting from others to get me going.

Opportunity Work - Questions & Exercises

What challenges/obstacles have you experienced/do

IDENTIFYING OBSTACLES AND CHALLENGES

you experience on your writing journey? How many are recurring or consistent?

Take a moment here to clarify what your obstacles and challenges might be. Write them down and include the first thing that comes to mind even if it doesn't make sense to you right now. It may very well make sense in hindsight.

How does your body respond to these obstacles? How does your mind respond?

What are your default behaviors when these obstacles come up? Emotionally? Physically? Mentally?

What is a new commitment you can make in service of keeping your creative road clear? What do you choose to do? All it takes is a choice.

Imagine a dear friend approaches you with the exact same feelings and experiences of obstacles. What would you tell them to encourage and support them? Now apply that brilliant advice to yourself!

CHAPTER 12
CREATING STRATEGY & POSSIBILITIES

Obstacles don't have to stop you. If you run into a wall, don't turn around and give up. Figure out how to climb it, go through it, or work around it.
Michael Jordan

Now that you've identified your usual obstacles and challenges, as well as how you've typically responded to them, let's create a new strategy for you!

An important lesson we've learned from coaching about self-assessment, goal setting and strategizing is that skills and strengths in one area of your life can be transferred to other areas of your life in which you'd like to genuinely see improvements. The idea is rather simple. Use what you know and tend to do well and apply it to other areas you've identified.

For example, if you struggle with time management, a possible strategy could be blocking off non-negotiable (and realistic) time blocks on your calendar to work on specific tasks or projects. This reminds you to not schedule anything else at that time.

If your obstacle is related to overwhelm, a possible strategy could be breaking down a huge aim into smaller, bite-sized steps. This helps you experience progress which in turn can boost your confidence.

If your obstacle is fear of criticism (see chapter nine), a possible strategy could be to ask yourself whether it's real or if it even matters. Be honest with yourself and, if you're having a hard time with this, consider giving yourself the advice you would give to a good friend in the same predicament.

Whatever your obstacle is, you already have the answers inside of you. Now is the time to name the many ways you can strategize in order to keep moving forward.

Use the opportunity work at the end of this chapter to help you formulate solutions and strategies that work for you using your own internal motivation and experience.

Author's Note from Anna

When I first started writing, I would often let myself feel overwhelmed by my obstacles before I put the first word onto paper. It was like trying to drive with the parking brake on. I became frustrated with the consistency of my challenge of overwhelm, so I decided one day to change my tack and face the factors head on. I realized I was often hungry when I sat down to write which meant I was having a hard time sustaining my focus and energy. Small gestures, such as having a snack before I sit down to write, or bringing a cup of tea to my desk so I could stay hydrated and warm made a big difference. I also scaled back my expectations and adjusted how much time I was willing to commit to writing every day. If the words were flowing, I kept going, but if I was experiencing a tough writing day, at least I showed up for it. Small tweaks can sometimes make a big difference!

Author's Note from Vindy

One of the obstacles I mentioned earlier in the book is the overwhelm I felt when thinking about all the steps it takes to publish a book: research, planning, writing, editing, formatting, publishing, and marketing. I was afraid I'd miss an important step or act on the wrong advice, thereby wasting my time or just getting it wrong. When I considered which transferable skills I could use from other areas of my life to overcome this obstacle, there was a very clear winner: I was a Planning & Organization Queen!

First, I needed a plan, and then I could organize my work and time around that plan. In exchange for breakfast at a wonderful local diner, one of my mentors offered to help me hammer out a book outline: 3 sections, 3 chapters in each, 3 main points in each one. It was easier than I thought once I focused on the big ideas and had sensible feedback from my *mentor. (See **Appendix** for the 3x3x3 Content Organization Tool).*

Though the final book was 20 chapters - clearly not divisible by 3 - the working outline I created in the diner that day served me well throughout the entire process. I could just pick a chapter or point, and just write on that.

Similarly, I broke up the writing and publishing steps and dealt with them one step at a time as well, regularly reminding myself that I need not have it all figured out from the start. If I came across something connected to a section I wasn't currently working on, I'd simply note it down for later and save it in a labeled file.

Finally, I learned to remain open to change if new information or resources became available, but reminded myself I didn't need to acquire a Ph.D. in every new thing that came up!

Opportunity Work - Questions & Exercises

What strategies have worked (or not worked) in the past in overcoming the challenges/obstacles you identified in the previous section? Write them all down and circle the ones that have worked for you, and cross out those that haven't.

Pick one or more (or all) of the obstacles you've identified in the previous chapter and fill in the sentence below. Let yourself think outside of the box - be creative with naming your solutions!

When I feel/think/experience__(obstacle)__, one way to overcome it is _____

Make a list of all the ways you've just written down to overcome your obstacles. You've just come up with a strategy that's tailor made to meet your needs! Keep this list handy to help you counteract obstacles and keep you moving forward. Stick it on your wall, post it on your desktop - keep it accessible. Remember you can always add to it as you discover new opportunities and insights. Let this be a living document to support your creativity.

What are some successful strategies you've used in other parts of your life? What are some new possibilities you can incorporate into your writing using the strategies you've identified? Add them to the list.

CHAPTER 13
WHEN IN DOUBT, KEEP GOING

Get it down. Take chances. It may be bad, but it's the only way you can do anything really good.
William Faulkner

If you are persistent, you will get it. If you are consistent, you will keep it.
Unknown

And by the way, everything in life is writable about if you have the outgoing guts to do it, and the imagination to improvise. The worst enemy to creativity is self-doubt.
Sylvia Plath

Once you start, momentum is key to keep those words flowing. If you are feeling stuck, put your fingers back onto the keyboard or pen to paper and let yourself write no matter what.

Although we may write in sprints, the creative process is a marathon. These epic races are not for the faint of heart. They require consistency, pace, and regular, persistent effort.

Even if you have no idea what to write about, you can write about that! Let yourself be creative in the ways you put words down every day.

Let yourself write about the limitations you experience, the writer's block, and lists of everything that you want to write about that you haven't yet put words to. Even in moments of feeling blocked, there is always a way through.

Earlier in this book we touched on the topic of making time to write, but it bears repeating. Many authors speak about the importance of writing every day. This may seem intimidating to some people, but all it requires is a choice. If you have a deadline or want to be done by a certain date, a daily writing practice will support you in reaching your goal and having a completed piece.

So how in the world do you keep yourself writing day in and day out?

A commitment to writing is a decision to show up no matter what. Carve out a regular time each day to write, even if all you're writing about is how you don't know what to write about!

When facing a challenge or setback that threatens to impede your creative process, or navigating different sized and shaped doubts, return to your WHY. Add to that the satisfaction and pleasure that comes with completing your writing piece, as well as the avoidance of the pain associated with not completing it. All of these things can provide much needed impetus and urgency that strengthen your resolve to keep going.

Most of us have experienced a variety of challenges and setbacks. They are a normal and expected part of life. Recognize them. Roll with them. It's your willingness to do this, and not give up, that can determine whether you'll reach a goal or not.

Author's Note from Vindy

In my book, I explore the "why" and "how" of momentum using two concepts: consistency and perseverance. Here's the short version! Consistency means putting in effort and practice to realize your goals. Even small, consistent efforts eventually add up to produce huge results. Perseverance is the determination shown in doing something despite difficulty or delay in achieving success. These two concepts are what allowed me to gain the momentum I needed to finish the first draft of my book in six months, and to continue working on it to completion, even when I experienced moments of tedium, frustration and fatigue.

OPPORTUNITY WORK - QUESTIONS & EXERCISES

What has been working for you? What hasn't been working? What can you adjust? Are there some tweaks you can make to your commitments for your writing practice (e.g., time of day, how long, where)?

Ideally, how much time would you like to write per day? How does that compare to where you are now?

Realistically, how much time would you like to write per day? How does that compare to where you are now?

All it takes to keep writing is a choice. What is a new commitment you can make in service of your writing practice? So, what do you choose to do?

If you have hit a block, ask yourself which other parts of the story you can work on. Just because the information is not flowing in one spot does not mean it can't flow in another. Give yourself permission to keep going with every aspect of the story, even if it means adding more description or....? Refer back to chapters eleven & twelve for additional techniques to identify obstacles and generate possibilities to continue writing.

PART FOUR: COMPLETING

*If you have a goal, write it down.
If you do not write it down, you do not have a goal—you
have a wish.*
Steve Maraboli

*Voice is not just the result of a single sentence or paragraph
or page. It's not even the sum total of a whole story. It's all
your work laid out across the table like the bones and fossils of
an unidentified carcass.*
Chuck Wendig

Completion is the home stretch!

To be done with your project and to have a fully written manuscript is a reason for celebration and joy. Sometimes, though, the process of completion can be fraught. Whether you feel self-doubt or are concerned about practical considerations, it will all come up as you approach completion.

Do not succumb to the doubts, discouraging voices, or practical hiccups. Completing a creative project can be a daunting idea for some. Remember it's always darkest before the light, and the same applies to the creative process. The successful end is in sight - you can do it!

In this part, we share some powerful tools and inspirations to help you reach completion.

CHAPTER 14
RE-ENGAGING WITH YOUR WHY

Storytelling is the way knowledge and understanding have been passed down for millennia, since long before the invention of written language. Storytelling is part of what it is to be human. And the best stories share our values and beliefs. Those stories are powerful. Those stories inspire. Those stories are both the source of our WHY and the fuel that keeps our WHY alive.
Simon Sinek

Tears are words that need to be written.
Paulo Coelho

I can shake off everything as I write; my sorrows disappear, my courage is reborn.
Anne Frank

As you prepare to complete your work, re-read what you've written through the lens of your WHY. Sometimes we can get hung up on the WHAT (our writing) and the HOW (however we write).

Why the WHY? Whatever yours is, it is the concept that got you writing in the first place. When we come back to it, we re-engage with the reason for beginning the project in the first place, and more importantly, our reason for finishing it. Take the time to re-engage with your WHY, and take it from there.

When we as writers circle back to why we are writing in the first place, we can make our piece a complete statement using that WHY. It provides a concise and satisfying reading experience. Pun intended: it bookends the piece!

Author's Note from Anna

When I was writing my book, my writing process was pretty chaotic. I would write a few paragraphs in one chapter, and then in another, and so on. I jumped around each day, writing what I could in each of the chapters.

When it came time to hand it over to my editor, I had what some people might call a "come to Jesus" moment. I was in a creatively very vulnerable place and was feeling very exposed as being a total joke. Why was I writing this, I asked myself, and why am I even doing this in the first place?

I sat with the question for a long time, and after a few days of chewing on it, my Why resurfaced and helped tie all the disparate pieces of my story together. It helped me see all the parts of my story not as separate continents but instead as an archipelago whose islands I got to connect to one another through my Great Big Why.

Had I not sat with the questions that were nagging me, I doubt I would have experienced such edifying clarity.

Opportunity Work - Questions & Exercises

Flip back to the Prologue and refresh your memory - what has kept your WHY alive? As you look through what you've written, have you stayed true to it? Are there any nuances or tones that you'd like to further speak into? Give yourself permission to add in whatever comes to mind as you hold the lens of your WHY while answering the following questions:

Why do you write?

What is your reason for this writing project? Have you stayed connected to it in your writing process? Can you reorient yourself toward your WHY as a way to move toward completion?

What is important to be included and/or considered in

your writing? Have you given it the attention and focus it deserves?

All it takes to complete your writing project is a choice. What is a new commitment you can make towards completing your writing? So, what do you choose to do?

CHAPTER 15
DIGGING DEEP

I started writing songs as a way to process and document my life. And a few years later music production became a way for me to hear those songs alive and in full form in the world. This record is about looking back at those ten years of work. It's about looking to the future by honoring the past… I wanted to give you the chance to hear me grow, hear me make mistakes, hear me change because all those pieces are all really beautiful parts of my present. And I don't feel complete without them in the world.

Maggie Rogers

When you're using language, you can create it and you can use it to divide people and build walls, or you can turn it into something where we can see each other more clearly as a bridge.

Ocean Vuong

We named this chapter Digging Deep because deeper levels of questioning, researching, or querying will bring more content, inspiration, and connection to your writing process and can help you over the finish line. It may not feel like a comfortable or convenient process, especially if you are impatient or want this to be done already. Be patient - the end is in sight!

This is where an investment of one more big push of energy to make it through will pay off handsomely.

To build upon the previous chapter, take a moment to reevaluate the following:

- **What is the purpose of this piece?** Has that been articulated clearly? What other supporting material can you bring in to materialize the purpose on the page?
- **What values are guiding you in this process?** What is the value of what you are working on? Play with rooting your writing in certain personal or collective values and make the connections clear and accessible.
- **What is your goal for your writing?** It is to educate, share, entertain, inspire, or…?
- **Is there any political, cultural or historical context that you can bring in to support what you are writing about?** This might

include shining a light on historically marginalized communities, underrepresented histories, or individual experiences within a greater context that can add depth and nuance? Think of this as zooming out from your focus to see what other contributing factors could help your piece come to life.
- **Could the story use more structure?** Or less?
- **What additional tools and resources can assist you in digging deeper?** Is there feedback and advice you can seek out? Please review the **Resource List** at the end of the book for guidance, direction and ideas.

The exercises below will encourage you to dig deep and uncover some of these nuggets.

Author's Note from Anna

I'm going to use an archaeology metaphor here. If you have ever seen an archaeologist at work, they systematically uncover one layer of ground at a time, a painstaking and dedicated endeavor. Whether they are using shovels, trowels, or a small brush that has only a handful of hairs to whisk away the smallest specks of dirt, the tools they use are all helping them to dig deep in service of the greater cause of discovery, restoration, realization, and illumination.

What tools do you have at your disposal to uncover the

hidden aspects of your story that may still be buried? What themes, elements, or events can you explore in depth in order to more clearly illuminate different corners of your story for the reader? Go deep - you may just find what you're looking for.

Opportunity Work - Questions & Exercises

What are the values, goals and purposes of, and for, your writing?

Identify familial, cultural, political, historical, psychological or other factors that inform your writing and writing goals.

Are there any other contexts or structures that may help tether your story?

Sit back and ask yourself what is missing, or what may help or support your story. Notice what comes to mind and let yourself play with it. It may be something you haven't yet considered, so be gentle with yourself as you uncover what next you get to include. Is there anyone you can interview to gain more depth, context, and nuance?

All it takes to complete your writing project is a choice. What is a new commitment you can make towards completing your writing? With that in mind, what do you choose to do?

CHAPTER 16
IMAGINING THE COMPLETION

Imagination is more important than knowledge.
Albert Einstein

Visualizing is daydreaming, with a purpose.
Bo Bennett

Everything you can imagine is real.
Pablo Picasso

The light at the end of the tunnel is in sight. Can you see it?

If you're up to your eyes in questions or challenges around completing your piece, imagining its completion can be one of the most powerful motivators in your creative writing process.

Be sure to spend some time creatively leaning into

the future, because one day you will be done with this. Just imagine what that will feel like!

- **Allow yourself time to dream, visualize and affirm your writing goals.** If you did this at the beginning of your journey, revisit what you wrote and notice what came to be. Are there any new, supportive thoughts or possibilities to bring in to help you complete this project?
- **Draw the front and back covers of your book.** Include rave reviews that will entice readers to buy your book.
- **Create a vision board or mind map** around how it will feel and what your life will look like once you are complete with this project.

A vision board is a collection of images and words, sometimes cut out of magazines, to act as a guide and landing pad for the ideas you want to bring into reality.

A mind map is a written out, non-linear list of ideas, themes and thoughts that you want to include. Mind maps are generally written out with no visual aids. They act like large nets to catch all of your ideas and wishes, no matter how big or small they are.

Both vision boards and mind maps can be visual aids to help you avoid distractions and serve as a running list of what brings you joy and satisfaction, or simply be easy motivational tools. We encourage you to be creative and let yourself play!

Author's Note from Vindy

If you're a perfectionist, or recovering perfectionists like Anna and I, then you may struggle with imagining the completion of your project. You might ruminate about what's missing, incomplete, or lacks depth. These party pooper worries quickly drain the motivation you might gain from vision boarding and mind mapping!

Allow me to share a concept that helped me complete my book about mindful living hacks. It's called the exploration vs. exploitation dilemma. I knew I had a lot of hacks to share but I was concerned I hadn't done exhaustive research and interviews (i.e., exploration). On the other hand, I already possessed a lot of relevant knowledge and wisdom that could readily help others and further my writing goals (i.e., exploitation). I realized that this could turn into a neverending struggle. I concluded that I would get the best results by balancing between exploiting my current knowledge (i.e., finishing and publishing my book) and continuing to explore the unknown (i.e., write future editions of the same book, new books, or do interviews and talks about additional knowledge and experience I acquired). For a recovering perfectionist, this was true progress!

Opportunity Work - Questions & Exercises

Take a moment to close your eyes and visualize being complete with this writing project. Notice what the weather is outside, where you are sitting, what you can see as you sit back in your chair and say to yourself "I did it."

How will you feel when you have finished this writing project? How will you see yourself? How will others see you?

How will you know when you've gotten there? Is there a desired word count, or a feeling in your gut? Or is there something else that will signal to you that you are done?

All it takes to complete your writing project is a choice. What is a new commitment you can make towards completing your writing? So, what do you choose to do?

Where do you need to call in support for completion? Do you need a proofreader? An editor? A publisher? A plan as to what comes next? These are all surmountable steps! Be clear about what you need and know that everything does not need to happen at once. Take it one step at a time, be clear about what you are looking for, and let yourself experience the joy of discovering solutions!

CONCLUSION

There is nothing more powerful than an idea whose time has come.
Victor Hugo (and Wayne Dyer)

A book is made from a tree. It is an assemblage of flat, flexible parts (still called "leaves") imprinted with dark pigmented squiggles. One glance at it and you hear the voice of another person, perhaps someone dead for thousands of years. Across the millennia, the author is speaking, clearly and silently, inside your head, directly to you. Writing is perhaps the greatest of human inventions, binding together people, citizens of distant epochs, who never knew one another. Books break the shackles of time--proof that humans can work magic.
Carl Sagan

Now more than ever, it is important to own our stories.

Your writing is valid, and your story belongs and matters just as much as the next person's.

Whether you're writing for yourself, close family and friends, or the public at large, we encourage you to keep going and make your writing available to those with whom you want to share it.

Let's destabilize the concept of a dominant narrative and show up for our stories, our lives, and our journeys. We never know who will read our writing, and there are untold numbers of people whose lives or journeys may be made a little bit easier through reading your story.

If you're just looking for a real-world reminder, consider what our friend Kriz Kozak has to say on the topic:

Behind every Netflix, Prime Video, or HBO movie, show or miniseries that are watched by gazillions of people... there are writers.

Behind every president's speech...there are writers.

Behind every late-night comedy show...there are writers.

Behind every conspiracy theory and propaganda spin... there are people who use their creativity to come up with this crap.

And behind every hit song...there are writers who came out with the lyrics.

It's cliché to say that we are story-telling creatures. But it is true...more than we can imagine.

It is our intention to support you and your creative endeavors. We hope that you found powerful insights, increased motivation, and practical tips within these pages to support your writing and creative expression.

We are passionate about helping people tell their story. If you want more support and resources, we encourage you to visit our site www.writingthroughtransition.com to learn more about us, our offerings, what past students have said, and to register for upcoming classes.

Here's to telling your story and writing, writing, writing!

With Encouragement,
 Anna & Vindy

ABOUT THE AUTHORS

Anna Brooke is a speaker, healing arts practitioner and author of the award-winning book *Stripped Down: How Burlesque Led Me Home*. She is also known as Rev. Legs Malone, a burlesque performer, show producer, educator and advocate of all things burlesque who has been featured in Page Six, Buzzfeed, and Huffington Post. www.annabrookehealing.com

Vindy Teja is a Professional Life & Divorce Coach, TEDx Speaker & Coach, and Author of the award-winning book, *YOLO: Essential Life Hacks for Happiness* and Co-author in *Passed Down from Mom* and *Inspiring True Stories of Everyday Heroes*. She is a graduate of The University of British Columbia and Western Law School. www.vindyteja.com

We welcome you to continue your writing journey and join us for our free Cornerstone Classes as well as our other classes. This includes our full Writing Through Transition workshop, where you will confidently be able to:

- Begin the book that lives inside you
- Metabolize major events through the written word
- Familiarize yourself with ways to share and publish your work
- Reclaim the narrative within your written legacy
- Bear witness to your unique journey

WRITING THROUGH TRANSITION is Vindy and Anna's collaboration that supports the process of self-expression through writing. Learn more at www.writingthroughtransition.com

ACKNOWLEDGMENTS

To Carrie Severson of The Unapologetic Voice House for publishing our first books and bringing us together. Thank you for showing us the way in.

To Candy Leigh, thank you for lighting the spark of conversation that led to our collaboration.

To all of our students and friends who so graciously test-read this little book of ours and provided valuable feedback and support. To Kris, Neeti, Audrey, Grace, Jillaine, T, Siobhan, Nelly, Kat, and Sally, THANK YOU!

To our friends, family and mentors for their patience, curiosity, and continuous encouragement.

We also want to acknowledge the silver lining of the pandemic that allowed our Writing Through Transition collaboration to seed and sprout. Without it, this book would not have been written.

APPENDIX

AFFIRMATIONS

Here is a list of affirmations that can be used to counteract blocks, limiting beliefs, or any fears that come up as a natural part of the writing process. This is far from being an exhaustive list - feel free to add your own!

Fear of failure → affirm success

- *I wrote x amount of words today and that is progress!*
- *I now choose to acknowledge my wins and successes of all shapes and sizes.*
- *When I write, I succeed.*

Fear of criticism → affirm the validation of your voice

- *I am brave to be writing from my heart.*

- *I am now ready/safe/willing to express my truth.*
- *My story is a powerful agent of change and support.*

Fear of rejection → affirm acceptance

- *The world is ready to read my story.*
- *I am ready to share my writing with the world.*
- *When I write, my words are received with gratitude.*

Fear of disappointment → affirm satisfaction

- *I now choose to celebrate my successes.*
- *I am now ready to feel satisfied with my efforts.*
- *I exceed everyone's expectations, including my own!*

Fear of being miserable → affirm contentment

- *I welcome in delight and pleasure from unexpected experiences.*
- *I am ready/willing/safe to acknowledge what feels good.*
- *I now allow myself contentment, pleasure, and enjoyment*

Fear of loneliness → affirm belonging

AFFIRMATIONS

- *My words and I are wanted and loved.*
- *My story belongs in the world.*
- *I am safe to connect and share my story.*

Fear of the unknown → affirm freedom and personal choice

- *I am safe to choose wisely for myself.*
- *I now welcome all conditions in alignment with my dreams/desires/purpose.*
- *I am free to choose what sets me up well as I move into the future.*

Fear of not knowing enough → affirm knowledge

- *I am safe/ready to share from what I know.*
- *I carry within me a wealth of knowledge.*
- *I trust that what I seek is within reach.*

Fear of not having enough to say → affirm enoughness

- *I am a walking, accessible encyclopedia of my lived experience.*
- *Words flow like water when I write.*
- *I now write from my enoughness.*

SELF-CARE TOOLS TO SUPPORT YOURSELF

- Be kind to yourself. Oftentimes our worst judges live in our own heads. Make a new decision to show up for you and your story and invite all parts of your head and heart in as allies in your creative process.

- If you've hit a wall, take a break. Get up, move around, get a glass of water or a snack, or do something different that mixes up your energy. Forcing yourself to be creative is a drag and not a creatively conducive state of mind.

- Keep going no matter what.

- Enlist the power of affirmations. There are thousands of ways to tackle unhelpful or limiting thoughts - let yourself be your own ally and enlist your brilliant mind to counteract any resistance that might be coming up. Use the power of your words to supersede any blocks that might stand in your way.

- To keep going, and to become your own ally in the creative process, identify chokepoints and then create new affirmations that counteract them and keep you writing. See above for a list of affirmations.

BRAINSTORM SHEET

A brainstorm is a creative exercise that helps you come up with new ideas and topics to write about. The list below is one we use in our online class to help students keep coming up with more content and stories.

Using the prompts below, write at least one association you have per category. Include events that are grounded in your life experience. Use this list as often as needed to generate new content, awareness, and written words.

Loss
Love
Parenthood
Childhood
Ancestor Stories
New Beginnings
Sudden Endings

BRAINSTORM SHEET

The First Time
The Last Time
Relocation/Moving
Health

3 X 3 X 3 CONTENT ORGANIZATION TOOL

This tool is to help you begin to brainstorm and organize the outline of your writing piece.

If it helps, think of this exercise as the bones of your piece which makes up a larger skeleton, upon which you can add muscles, nerves and flesh as your writing progresses.

Start with your three main themes, or parts (A, B, C). Under each one, write down three chapter titles or section headings (1, 2, 3). Under each of those chapters or sections, write three topics which can include events/stories, points, or takeaways that pertain to the chapter or section.

Theme/Part A

- Chapter/Section 1
  - Topics covered (1-3)
- Chapter/Section 2
  - Topics covered (1-3)
- Chapter/Section 3
  - Topics covered (1-3)

Theme/Part B
- Chapter/Section 4
  - Topics covered (1-3)
- Chapter/Section 5
  - Topics covered (1-3)
- Chapter/Section 6
  - Topics covered (1-3)

Theme/Part C
- Chapter/Section 7
  - Topics covered (1-3)
- Chapter/Section 8
  - Topics covered (1-3)
- Chapter/Section 9
  - Topics covered (1-3)

Remember, you can move around, expand, repeat, or remove any of the parts as you go.

For example, you can add further themes, sections, chapters, topics, points, and subpoints.

The point here is to use structure as an ally to organize your writing…and your own creativity and intelligence!

RESOURCE LIST

Here is a list of the links we love, use, and have mentioned in the book.

Structuring your story:

https://education.nationalgeographic.org/resource/elements-storytelling

https://www.aresearchguide.com/genres-of-writing.html

Fiction Writing :

https://www.newyorker.com/humor/daily-shouts/eight-rules-for-writing-fiction

https://writers.com/writing-tips

https://writers.com/how-to-start-writing-fiction

Short Story Writing:

https://blog.reedsy.com/guide/short-story/how-to-write-a-short-story/

Film and Speech Beatsheets:

https://boords.com/blog/how-to-write-a-beat-sheet-free-template#beat-sheet-examples

News Articles:

https://www.wikihow.com/Write-a-News-Article

Classic Storytelling Techniques:

https://www.sparkol.com/en/blog/8-classic-storytelling-techniques-for-engaging-presentations

Memoir Writing:

https://www.masterclass.com/articles/how-to-start-writing-a-memoir

Creativity:

Here is an article Vindy contributed to on tips for tapping into your creativity.

https://www.weightwatchers.com/ca/en/article/how-tap-your-creativity

Vision Boarding:

https://www.shewrites.com/blog/view/2873194/why-vision-boards-are-a-killer-tool-for-wannabe-writers

Mindset:

https://hiddenbrain.org/podcast/reframing-your-reality-part-1/ https://hiddenbrain.org/podcast/reframing-your-reality-part-2/

Mind Map link

https://www.mindmapping.com

And don't forget about your best resource - **YOU!**

Vindy's and Anna's books:

https://www.vindyteja.com/yolo-essential-life-hacks-for-happiness/

http://www.annabrookehealing.com/stripped-down

Our website:

www.writingthroughtransition.com